FLOORED! SUPERCARS

MERCEDES-BENZ

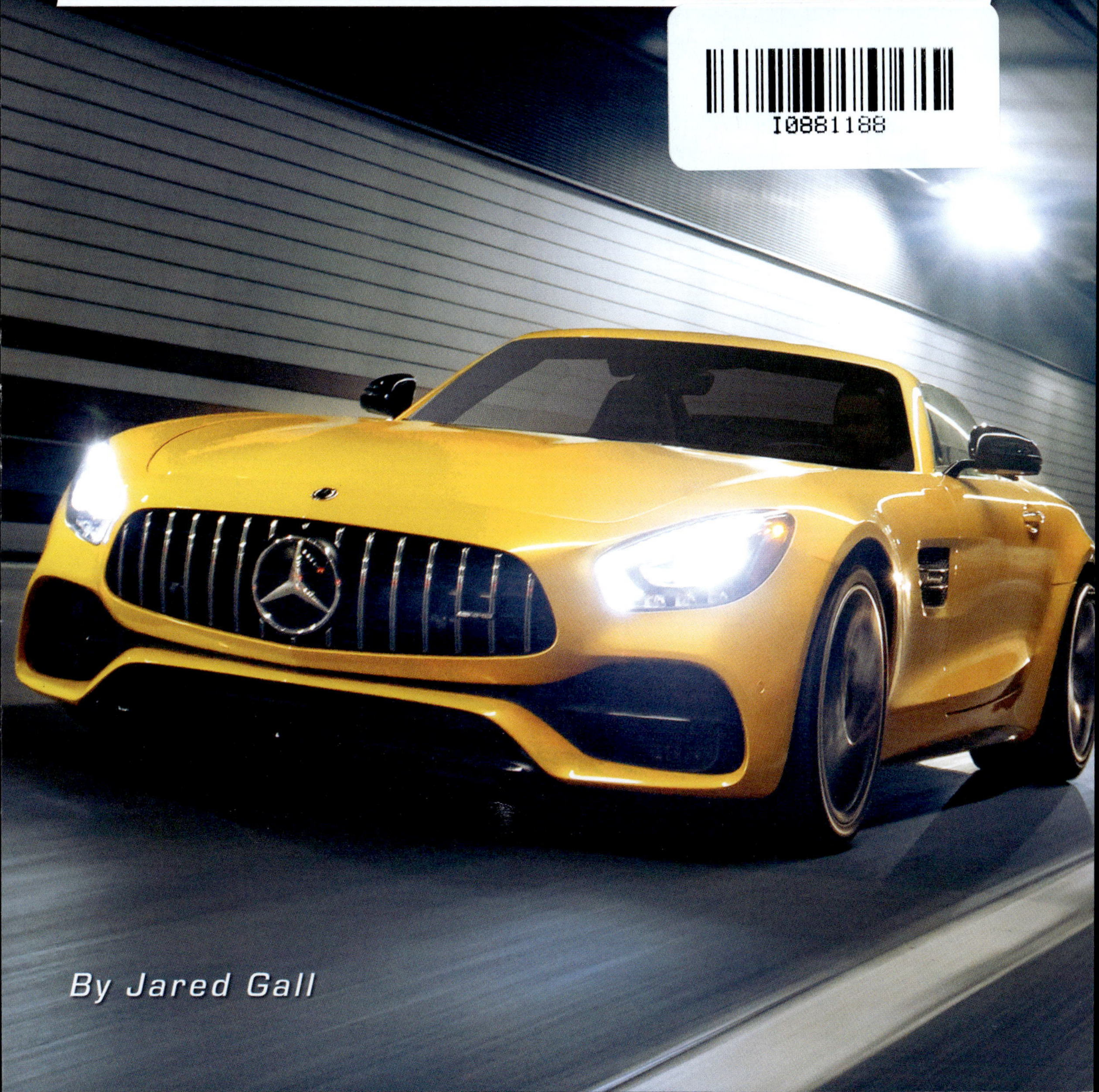

By Jared Gall

45TH PARALLEL PRESS

Published in the United States of America by Cherry Lake Publishing Group
Ann Arbor, Michigan
www.cherrylakepublishing.com

Reading Adviser: Beth Walker Gambro, MS, Ed., Reading Consultant, Yorkville, IL

Photo Credits: © Ethan Yetman/Shutterstock, cover, title page; © SamKal/Shutterstock, 3; © Camerasandcoffee/Shutterstock, 4; © Ethan Yetman/Shutterstock, 6–7; © ClassicCarPhoto/Shutterstock, 8; © Sergei Afanasev/Shutterstock, 10; © Dmitry Eagle Orlov/Shutterstock, 11; © Zavatskiy Aleksandr/Shutterstock, 12–13; © Jay Hirano/Shutterstock, 14; © Evgeniyqw/Shutterstock, 16; Neil, CC BY 2.0 via Wikimedia Commons, 18–19; © Ethan Yetman/Shutterstock, 20; © Roman.Stasiuk/Shutterstock, 22–23; © Veyron Photo/Shutterstock, 24; © teddyleung/iStock, 26; NearEMPTiness, CC BY-SA 4.0 via Wikimedia Commons, 28–29; © Sergey Kohl/Dreamstime.com, 30 (top); © FernandoV/Shutterstock, 30 (bottom); © VanderWolf Images/Shutterstock, 31 (top); © Veyron Photo/Shutterstock, 31 (bottom)

45th Parallel Press is an imprint of Cherry Lake Publishing Group.

Library of Congress Cataloging-in-Publication Data has been filed and is available at catalog.loc.gov.

Printed in the United States of America

Note from Publisher: Websites change regularly, and their future contents are outside of our control. Supervise children when conducting any recommended online searches for extended learning opportunities.

ABOUT THE AUTHOR:

Jared Gall writes about cars and trucks for magazines and websites. He has driven everything from semitrucks and school buses to sports cars and supercars. He has raced off-road buggies through the desert in Mexico and Mercedes-Benzes on frozen lakes in Sweden. He has driven a lot of Mercedes-Benzes, but never an AMG One. His personal top speed is 189 miles (304.2 kilometers) per hour, set while driving a Ferrari.

Table of Contents

Most supercars are custom-made. People pay for special features.

CHAPTER 1

Introduction

There are many kinds of cars. They're good at different things. Minivans have lots of space. Whole families can fit. They can ride together to school. They can ride together on vacation. **Sport utility vehicles** are called SUVs. They also have lots of space. They're made to tow heavy things. They tow boats. They tow campers. They also go off-roading.

Sports cars are built to be fast. They're fun to drive. They're small. They're light. This makes them **agile**. Agile means they can turn quickly and easily. They go around corners fast.

Supercars are like sports cars. But they go even faster. Their engines have more power. They're lighter. They go faster on straight roads. They turn faster. Many are built with special metal. This makes them extra light.

Most supercars sit low. They're close to the ground. This makes them **aerodynamic**. That means they move through air easily. Imagine putting your hand out a car window. Imagine facing your palm into the wind. It would be hard to keep your hand still. But what if you lay your hand flat? It would then be easier to hold your hand steady. Your hand is more aerodynamic when it's flat. Being aerodynamic makes supercars fast.

Have you ever seen a Mercedes-Benz? Have you seen one on the road? If so, then you have seen a supercar! Mercedes-Benzes are special. Let's learn more!

The Mercedes-Benz CLK GTR was developed in only 128 days. That's only a little more than 4 months!

Classic Mercedes-Benz cars can still be found all over the world! This one races through Italy in the Mille Miglia race.

CHAPTER 2

Mercedes-Benz History

Mercedes-Benz is a very old company. Two companies joined to create it. One company was started by 2 men. Their names were Gottlieb Daimler and Wilhelm Maybach. The other company was started by Carl Benz.

All 3 men were **engineers**. Engineers design things. They build things. These men were also **pioneers**. Pioneers do things before others. They take risks. They invent new ways of doing things. Benz built his first engine in 1879. Daimler and Maybach built their first engine in 1884. Cars didn't exist yet.

Daimler and Maybach built the world's first motorcycle. The first one was made of wood. That was in 1885. Benz invented the car. He did this in 1886. This was the world's first car.

Lots of people didn't think cars were safe. People used horses to go places back then. They didn't trust cars. They thought horses were better than cars.

Benz's wife was named Bertha. Bertha Benz took charge. She and her sons took the world's first road trip. She drove to see her mom. Her mom lived 62 miles (99.8 kilometers) away. That is not far today. But it was far in 1888. People were amazed. They were willing to give cars a try.

The first car had only 3 wheels. It was called a motor wagon.

The first Mercedes-Benz car was the Type 630.

People started racing cars. This happened soon after cars were invented. These early race cars were fast for back then. We wouldn't think they were fast today. A very slow modern car could beat an early car.

Daimler and Maybach built race cars. They did this for a rich man. His name was Emil Jellinek. Jellinek helped sell the race cars. He named one of the cars Mercedes. He named it after his daughter. Daimler and Maybach started to call all of their cars Mercedes.

Daimler died in 1900. Maybach left and started his own company in 1907. Daimler's company and Carl Benz became partners in 1924. They created a company called Daimler-Benz. It built the first Mercedes-Benz car in 1926. The company became Mercedes-Benz Group in 2022. Mercedes-Benz now owns Maybach. It uses the name for its most expensive cars. Maybachs are very fancy.

The Mercedes-Benz logo is a star. The star has 3 points. It's surrounded by a wreath. Daimler's sons designed the logo. They did this in 1909. The Mercedes-Benz logo is actually older than the company!

A 2016 Mercedes-Benz Maybach 6 concept car

Lewis Hamilton was the youngest #1 F1 driver. He was 15.

Behind the Wheel

Lewis Hamilton is a champion. He's won more F1 races than any other driver. F1 stands for **Formula 1**. It's a race. F1 cars are fast race cars. He's won 103 races. That's 12 more than Michael Schumacher. Schumacher is another F1 driver. He's won the second-most races. Hamilton has won twice as many races as Max Verstappen. Verstappen is the third-most successful F1 driver.

Hamilton gets a lot of attention. He's the best F1 driver in history. He's also the only Black Fl driver. He uses this attention to promote racial justice. *Drive to Survive* is a TV show. It's on Netflix. It's about F1. Hamilton was on it. He said, "When you have all that success, what are you going to do with it? I'm not going to win all these championships and have all this success and not use it to make change."

The 300SL was featured at the New York International Auto Show in 1954. It was a hit.

CHAPTER 3

Mercedes-Benz Evolution

Mercedes-Benz built the 300SL. This happened in 1954. Many think the 300SL is the first supercar. The 300SL was based on a race car. The race car was also called the 300SL. The 300SL supercar could go 161 miles (259.1 km) per hour. That made it the world's fastest car.

Metal bars surrounded the driver and passenger in the 300SL. The bars made it safer. But the bars were where doors should be. Engineers raised the doors. They made doors open up, instead of out. These are called gullwing doors. A gull is a bird. The doors look like bird wings. Many supercars today have gullwing doors.

Mercedes-Benz built the 300SL only for a few years. But the company kept working on it. It made it faster. It changed the name to 300SLR. It built only 2 of them. These cars are also called 300 SLR Uhlenhaut Coupés. **Coupes** are cars with 2 seats.

These cars were named after their designer. His name was Rudolf Uhlenhaut. Mercedes-Benz still has one of them. It's in a museum. It sold the other one in 2022.

Mercedes-Benz built the C111. This happened in 1969. The C111 was an experiment. Mercedes-Benz used the C111 to test different engines. It never sold any of them. The C111 was a **mid-engine**. That means the engine was behind the driver. The engine is in the front in most cars. Mid-engines made cars faster.

The 300 SLR Uhlenhaut Coupé sold for $143 million. It's the most expensive car ever.

Mercedes-Benz built 28 CLK GTRs. One sold for $10.2 million in 2023.

Mercedes-Benz had never built a mid-engine road car before. It had built mid-engine race cars. But race cars are very different from road cars. Race cars need to be fast. Road cars need more. They need to be comfortable. They need to be safe. They need to be **efficient**. Efficient means not wasting energy. Efficient cars can go far before needing gas.

AMG is another car company. AMG **modified** Mercedes-Benz cars. Modify means to change. AMG helped build the CLK GTR. It did this in 1997. The CLK GTR was a race car. It could be driven on public roads. It was the first mid-engine Mercedes-Benz. It was also the first Mercedes-Benz supercar since the 300SL. In 1999, Mercedes-Benz bought AMG.

Fast Facts

Mercedes-Benz and AMG build lots of special cars. But they built only a few of each of these:

- AMG called its first race car the Red Pig. Race cars are small. They're light. The Red Pig was big. It was heavy. But it was very fast.
- Mercedes-Benz used to build minivans. They were called the R-class. The company also built a fast version. It was called the R63. The R63 had a supercar engine. It could go 155 miles (249.4 km) per hour. Mercedes-Benz built only about 200 R63s.
- Mercedes-Benz also builds off-road trucks. These are called the G-class. The company built a 6-wheeled G-class. The truck is called the G63 6x6. It has huge tires. It's more than 7 feet (2.1 meters) tall.
- Mercedes-Benz also built a convertible version of the G-class. It called it the G650 Landaulet. *Landaulet* is another word for "convertible."

The next Mercedes-Benz supercar was the SLR. Mercedes-Benz built engines for McLaren F1 race cars. McLaren helped Mercedes-Benz build the SLR. The car was called the Mercedes-McLaren SLR. A version with no windshield or roof was built. It was named the SLR Stirling Moss. Stirling Moss was a British race car driver. He won many famous races. He drove the 300SLR.

Mercedes-Benz kept building supercars. Their next one was the SLS. The SLS looked like the 300SL. It had gullwing doors. It could go 197 miles (317 km) per hour. A special version of the SLS was built. It was called the Black Series. It had a big wing on the back. This wing created more **downforce**. Downforce is when air pushes the car against the ground. This helps cars take turns faster. There was also an electric SLS. It was called the SLS Electric Drive.

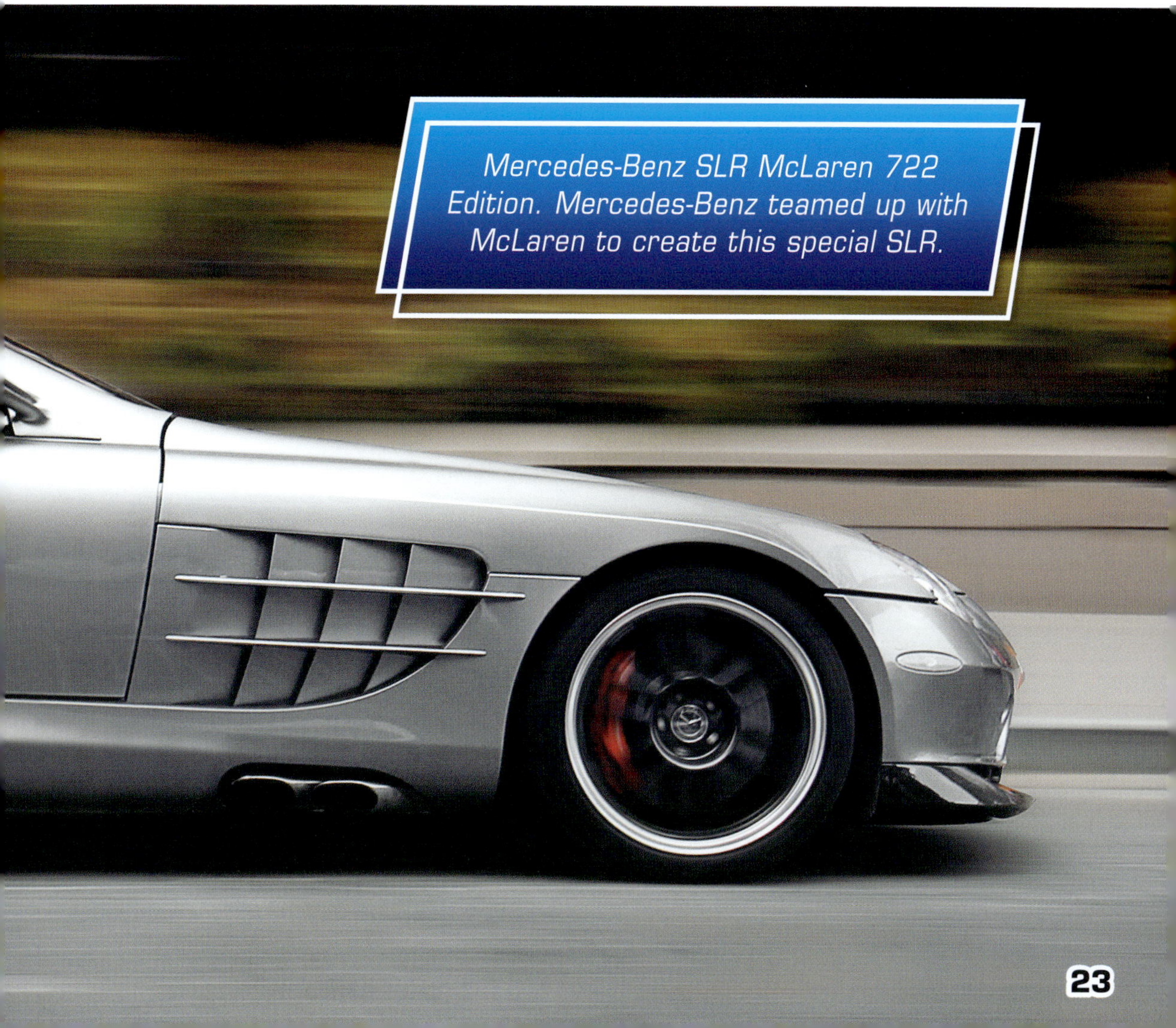

Mercedes-Benz SLR McLaren 722 Edition. Mercedes-Benz teamed up with McLaren to create this special SLR.

Mercedes offers 3 engines in the AMG GT: fast, faster, and fastest.

CHAPTER 4

Mercedes-Benz Today

Mercedes-Benz builds **luxury** cars. Luxury means fancy. AMG makes faster versions of most Mercedes-Benz cars. But there isn't a slow version of the AMG GT. Every AMG GT is a supercar. The fastest AMG GT is a **hybrid**. Hybrid cars have a gas engine and an electric motor.

Electric motors make cars more efficient. They help cars go faster. The AMG GT can drive short distances on just the electric motor. That means it doesn't burn any gas. It can go from 0 to 60 miles (0 to 96.6 km) per hour. It does this in 2.7 seconds. A normal car needs 8 seconds to do that. The GT can go almost 200 miles (321.9 km) per hour.

The AMG GT is costly. There's a version that isn't a hybrid. It costs $136,000. The hybrid costs $200,000. You could buy 5 normal cars for that much.

Mercedes-Benz also builds all-electric cars. This series of electric cars are called EQ. These cars don't have gas engines. Like cell phones, they have batteries. But their batteries are way bigger. Electric cars don't need gas. They are plugged into electrical outlets instead. That recharges the batteries.

The EQ cars have the longest range. They travel farther than other electric cars. They don't need to be charged as often.

Electric cars are very quick. The Mercedes-Benz EQS is an electric **sedan**. Sedans have roofs. They seat at least 4 people. The EQS can go from 0 to 60 miles (0 to 96.6 km) per hour in 3.5 seconds. That's very fast for a big luxury car. The company also makes the EQE. It's even faster. It goes from 0 to 60 miles (0 to 96.6 km) per hour in 3.2 seconds.

The EQE is another Mercedes-Benz EQ.

Cost of Ownership

MODEL	PRICE
2024 Toyota Camry	$27,500
2024 Honda CR-V	$31,000
2024 Ford F-150	$39,000

MODEL	PRICE
2024 Mercedes-Benz AMG GT	$135,000
2024 Mercedes-Benz AMG GT hybrid	$200,000
2024 Mercedes-Benz EQE	$107,000
2024 Mercedes-Benz EQS	$147,500
Mercedes-Benz G63 6x6	$511,000
Mercedes-Benz G650 Landaulet	$550,000
Mercedes-Benz AMG One	$2,700,000

The AMG One takes less than 3 seconds to go from 0 to 60 miles (0 to 96.6 km) per hour. It's a supercar. It's a mid-engine. Supercar engines tend to be similar to company's race car engines. But the AMG One is different. It uses a real F1 engine. It has a **turbocharger**. A turbocharger is a small fan. The fan is attached to an engine. It blows air into the engine. This helps engines make more power. The AMG One is a hybrid. It's the fastest Mercedes-Benz ever.

The **Nürburgring** is a famous racetrack in Germany. Car companies take sports cars and supercars there. They time their

laps. They brag about how fast their cars are. The AMG One set the all-time record for a supercar. Mercedes-Benz built only 275. They cost $2.7 million each. Three of them were sold to F1 drivers.

Car companies are always making their cars better. They make luxury cars more comfortable. They make efficient cars more efficient. And they make supercars faster. Someday, Mercedes-Benz will make a faster car than the AMG One. Maybe you will drive one someday!

The Mercedes-Benz AMG One is an F1 car for the road.

Timeline of a Legend

1879 — Carl Benz builds his first engine.

1886 — Carl Benz builds the world's first car.

1901 — The Mercedes name first appears on a car.

1926 — The first Mercedes-Benz car is made.

1954 — The Gullwing 300SL comes out.

1969

Mercedes-Benz builds the C111. This is its first mid-engine car.

1997

The CLK GTR comes out.

1999

Mercedes-Benz buys AMG.

2010

The SLS is introduced.

2022

Mercedes-Benz builds the AMG One. This is its fastest car ever.

Find Out More

BOOKS

Adkins, Jan. *Bertha Takes a Drive: How the Benz Automobile Changed the World.* Watertown, MA: Charlesbridge, 2017.

Sanchez Vegara, Maria Isabel. *Little People, Big Dreams: Lewis Hamilton.* London, United Kingdom: Frances Lincoln Children's Books, 2023.

WEBSITES

Search these online sources with an adult:

Mercedes-Benz Facts for Kids | Kiddle

Mercedes-Benz | Academic Kids

Glossary

aerodynamic (air-oh-dye-NAA-mik) able to move easily through the air

agile (A-juhl) able to change direction quickly

coupes (KOOPS) 2-door cars that usually seat 2 people

downforce (DOWN-fors) a downward aerodynamic force

efficient (ih-FIH-shuhnt) able to be more productive with less energy

engineers (en-juh-NEERZ) people who design and build things

Formula 1 (FOR-myuh-luh WUHN) a racing series with the fastest race cars in the world; also called F1

hybrid (HYE-bruhd) a car with a gasoline engine and an electric motor

luxury (LUHK-shuh-ree) something that is not necessary but makes people happy or comfortable

mid-engine (mid-EN-juhn) having the engine behind the driver

modified (MAH-duh-fyd) changed or improved

Nürburgring (NUR-ber-gruhng) a famous racetrack in Germany

pioneers (pye-uh-NEERZ) people who are the first to do or invent something

sedan (sih-DAN) a car with 2 to 4 doors that seats at least 4 people

sport utility vehicles (SPORT yoo-TIH-luh-tee VEE-uh-kuhlz) vehicles designed to be used on rough surfaces but often used on city streets; also called SUVs

supercars (SOO-per-kahrz) cars designed to go faster than other cars

turbocharger (TER-boh-char-juhr) a small fan that blows air into the engine and produces more power

Index